MARITAL BLISS
UNLOCKED

Nuggets for Upgrading Romance in your Marriage

Adesina Okerinde & Mosebolatan Akande

MARITAL BLISS UNLOCKED

Nuggets for Upgrading Romance in your Marriage

Copyright © 2019 by **Adesina Okerinde & Mosebolatan Akande**

ISBN: 978-1-944652-88-3

Cornerstone Publishing
Phone: +1(516) 547-4999
info@thecornerstonepublishers.com
www.thecornerstonepublishers.com

Conect with the authors:

Instagram: @shynapokky
Email: shn24@yahoo.com
Facebook: Adesina David Okerinde

Instagram: @arinshyna
Email: arinakande@yahoo.com
Facebook: Arin Akande-Crown

This publication may not be reproduced, stored in a retrieval system, or transmitted in whole or in part, in any form or by any means, electronic, mechanical, photocopying, recording, or otherwise, without the prior written permission of the publisher.
All rights reserved.

Printed in United States of America

Dedication

To the source of knowledge, the greatest Author Himself, the Almighty God.

Acknowledgments

We want to appreciate our lovely kids, Olamide, Pappy, and Fikayomi. You all have been a source of inspiration for us. Thanks for the love guys.

Despite his very busy schedule and living in another country, our daddy, Professor Samuel Oyetunji Akande, took time to read the manuscripts of the book and gave professional inputs. Thank you so much daddy. We appreciate the love.

We also want to appreciate my dear friend, Olanrewaju Olayiwola for the tips and guides all through the years while writing the book. Thanks buddy.

Thank you Adeyinka Adegoke for being there through the years and most importantly for helping us to find a suitable publisher for this book.

We also want to appreciate Ola Aboderin who volunteered to edit the book. Thank you, sir.

And to the amazing publishing team of The Cornerstones Publishing led by Pastor Gbenga Showumi, thank you for the amazing job. God bless you.

And most importantly, thanks to the Almighty God for the inspiration, provision of resources and knowledge. You are the greatest author of all time.

Contents

Dedication..5
Acknowledgments.......................................7
Introduction...11

1. Specifically Unlocked............................13

2. Romantically Unlocked..........................35

3. Compromisingly Unlocked....................47

4. Thoughtfully Unlocked..........................71

INTRODUCTION

Everything in life is guided by specific principles, and the earlier we understand the principles guiding the marital institution, the better for our homes. With years of marital experience and divine inspiration, Marital Bliss Unlocked has unlocked some deep thought-provoking principles that can guide and help homes to enjoy a blissful experience.

The book is divided into different compartments. Marriage, like any other relationships, starts with self before it is extended to one's partner. The Specifically

Unlocked section highlighted some important principles of what individuals need to take note of while in a relationship or before venturing into one. The Romantically Unlocked section gave crucial tips on the benefits of being romantically connected to one's partner. The Compromisingly Unlocked section puts the spotlight on nagging marital issues that if handled without aforehand knowledge of its implications can degenerates badly and wreck homes. The Thoughtfully Unlocked section is filled with instructions that can help couples navigate through their marital huddles.

Marriage is designed to be enjoyed and not to be endured. We believe Marital Bliss Unlocked will help you to experience peace in your homes.

SPECIFICALLY UNLOCKED

"A heart broken by love can only be healed by love." — ADO

A heart broken by love can only be mended by love

Ego is one of the greatest threats to the peace of any marriage.

The easiest way to earn another person's respect is by respecting yourself.

Neither age nor academic degree is a qualification for having a good marriage.

A lot of married people haven't developed the courage to love.

Some marriages are one nasty attitude away from divorce. Everything isn't spiritual.

Don't let the ego of "what will people say?" keep you in an abusive relationship.

If you make a list of your spouse's offenses to you, you will find out that most of them are filled with your personal ego.

Did you marry the wrong person, or you are just the wrong person?

If you haven't learnt how to be by yourself, you can't master how to be by anyone.

You are not a fool for trusting your spouse; they are rather irresponsible for betraying your trust.

The moment you demand for respect, you automatically lose the respect you have earned earlier

You mock every beautiful home and wonder why you don't have a beautiful one. You can't become what you mock. It is that simple.

Love is never a function of age. It is a function of the mind. You can find love at any age and time of your life.

You are the space between your dreams and the reality. You are your own future.

You can never fully appreciate the power of mentorship until the day you try to explore an opportunity no one has explored before.

We pray daily not to be locked up in jail, but what of being mentally incarcerated by a rigid mindset?

No matter how smart you are, if you associate with toxic people for too long, you will eventually become toxic.

To be free from an abusive relationship, you must be financially independent. You are a slave to whoever is feeding you.

Never let any helping hands leave you bitter. That someone once helped you doesn't mean you should become their slave.

Being a good spouse has more to do with personality than with the marriage institution. It is difficult to be a self-righteous person and still be a good spouse.

When you become an invaluable resource to your wife, it becomes difficult for her to disrespect you. Women naturally worship great leaders.

Husband as a provider is never limited to providing food. A good husband provides wisdom, counseling and, most importantly, friendship and peace at home. God doesn't provide fruits; He provides the seeds and the field.

Having a good heart will always supersede having a good face. No matter how ugly you might think you are, people will still find something cute about you if your heart is good.

If you must impress anyone to value your friendship, my friend, you are in the wrong relationship. You can never ever struggle to command the attention of the one that truly loves you.

No one makes a sane decision from a bitter mind.

Patience is part of the pathway to greatness.

Whether male or female, marriage should never make anyone feel less a human being.

There is no weapon on earth as powerful and as weak as the mind.

The opinion you support and agree with has a say on what you will become eventually in life.

You can't aspire for greatness and avoid the spotlight from shining on you.

You can't have all the beautiful things in life, but you can make everything you have in life to be beautiful

Don't let your mind be a dumping ground for mediocrity. Always sieve out the truth.

If you can't be at peace with anyone in life, please, at least, be at peace with yourself.

The fact that you express a bad attitude on some occasions doesn't make you a bad person. We all have our low moments. Pick up and move on.

The people with an annoying attitude in your life that you think will change might not change until you change your attitude. Sometimes, God uses the annoying situations to build us and get the best out of us.

Sometimes you go through painful moments, not because you are not smart enough to outwit it but just to teach you how to look at people in the valley with humility.

Before you get jealous of another man's blessings, take time to count yours.

Just as the most important piece on the chessboard is the one being pushed at every moment, so also the most important decision of your life is the one you are making right now. Be calculative, be thoughtful, and be dutiful. It is your life, live it smartly.

ROMANTICALLY UNLOCKED

"If you treat your wife as a queen, that automatically makes you a king." — MAA

Just as lots of men love sex, affection brightens the day of a woman.

Being romantic is never out of fashion in marriage. Don't ever stop being your spouse's Romeo or Juliet.

Good sex doesn't guarantee a good marriage, but, with one, there is a chance he/she won't let you go easily

---

Education on good hygiene is what some spouses need, not prayer vigil.

A sexually starved spouse is usually a frustrated spouse.

The period of dating never ends on the wedding day. It is continuous till death. Learn to date your spouse again and again.

Your primary responsibility in a marriage is your spouse, not the kids. The kids joined the party later. If your spouse is happy, it will automatically reflect on the kids.

If you treat your wife as a queen, that automatically makes you a king.

Dining together with your spouse is another bonding moment.

———◄○►———

Gossiping with your spouse creates friendship bond

To know your spouse again might require you to re-date them.

Getting angry with a spouse that is not angry with you paves ways for frustration.

Don't think that keeping quiet when your spouse hurts you will keep tension away from your marriage. No, you are only postponing the day of evil. If it hurts you enough for you to think about it all the time, let them know they hurt you.

Marriage has no immunity for anger. It provides a breeding ground to express anger. Fix it before it breaks you.

If you turn your kids against your spouse during a moment of argument, you might spend eternity trying to turn them for him/her when the fight is over.

There may be exceptions, but most women want their husbands to show them off.

No matter how long your courtship lasts, you will always learn something new about each other.

Unity in marriage is a form of spiritual armor.

COMPROMISINGLY UNLOCKED

"Marriage will be fun, if we take it as the extension of friendship."
— ADO

We will enjoy it better, if we take marriage as the extension of friendship.

Every marriage has a specific rule that works for its success. Every couples must create theirs.

A wise man works to earn his wife's respect, a foolish man fights to demand for his wife's submission.

A successful marriage is never a measure of how rich the couple are, but how peaceful the home is.

You can't demand for someone's attention and be stingy with yours.

It is okay to learn from other people's marriages, but it is criminal to compare your marriage with those of others.

Don't confuse your role as a spouse with that of a porter. You can't change anyone.

Never give your spouse the opportunity to always doubt you. Lack of trust is a threat to the peace of any relationship.

Whatever principle you decide to follow eventually, marriage is never designed to make your life miserable.

The danger is investigating your spouse is that you will always find fault. Knowing your spouse is learning how to love them better, investigating them is finding fault.

The more rigid you are in a marriage, the higher your chances of being frustrated. Being flexible will cut half of your headaches about marriage. Think about it for a sec.

Some of your divorced and single friends will advise you to leave your marriage, just to prove that no marriage can work. Misery loves company

If God hasn't made your marriage complicated, don't complicate things by attracting unnecessary drama into your home.

Don't draw bad conclusions about marriage because of the failure of some; there are beautiful and cool marriages out there.

No matter how good you are at praying, you can't pray away every annoying situation. Some, you just have to deal with.

If you hold on too tight to your spouse, you stand a chance of losing them. Just let them be themselves; if they are truly yours, they will be. And if they are not yours, they are just not yours. Love them the best way you can and hope for the best. Don't make an already difficult life more difficult for yourself

It is not everybody that asks for your trouble that actually deserves it. The only reason why some people hang around you is just to trigger your error. Let them wait for a while.

Even if your in-laws couldn't give you all the support you expected on your wedding day, at least, they gave you their child. You already got the bargain of the day. Move on!

The biggest gift you could get on your wedding day is your spouse saying, "I do". Walk away with it!

Privacy in marriage never overrules transparency.

Learn to differentiate between an overprotective in-law and a bad in-law. You don't know how many pillows they have soaked with tears to get your spouse ready for this moment.

That you hate your in-laws doesn't mean your spouse must hate them too.

You pick your spouse; your kids pick you. That proves to you that you don't have power over everything in marriage.

Marriage is a journey, not a moment. And being equipped with the best GPS won't take away potholes from the roads. There are bound to be rough moments in every home.

If you can't behave around your spouse the way you would have behaved when you are by yourself, then your marriage needs help.

Most times, it is not our complains that our spouses turn down, it is our method of delivery that further worsens the issue.

The fact that you are talking to your spouse doesn't mean you are communicating with them. Most times, we only condemn them rather than making our complaints known.

Behind the scene of the production of a good marriage, there is tolerance, patience, and compromise working tirelessly to make sure the show gets to the limelight. Even a marriage that is made in heaven still must be formed on earth

It is not cowardice to walk out of a relationship that has the intention of walking you out of life.

Fulfilling purpose becomes difficult when you compete against the people you are supposed to bring into your team.

If you don't learn to understand the language of your spouse, they can be screaming for help right beside you and you won't understand a single word of what they are saying until the relationship crumbles to the sea.

If you already know that it is poisonous, there is no need to check if it smells good.

In marriage, your complaints should focus more on correcting the errors, not condemning your spouse. Unfortunately, we are expert at the latter.

Not everyone that corrects you hates you. And not everyone that praises you adores you.

Accountability is a major key in marriage. Once you are married, you are accountable to someone and someone is accountable to you.

Not all facts are applicable to all situations.

There is a difference between listening to your spouse to understand their pains and listening to them just to build a good case against them.

Nothing insults a man's ego than to abuse him with his failures, especially if his peers succeed where he has tried and failed.

Falling in love is pediatric, sustaining the relationship is where maturity is being put to test.

It is beautiful to give everything to your spouse, but it is even more rewarding if they are built not to wait for you to get it because, on the days of your insanity, their dignity might be the only thing that will keep you sane.

That someone betrayed your trust in a marriage doesn't mean you are a fool. However, you join the fools' party the moment you resort to domestic violence just to revenge.

Just because your spouse talks softly doesn't mean they are not serious with what they are complaining about.

Don't expect your spouse to solve your problem; they are carrying theirs. It is God that solves problems.

Having an educated and intelligent spouse relives one of some marital stress.

THOUGHTFULLY UNLOCKED

"A peaceful marriage is another form of nourishment to the soul".
— ADA

If you are strong, build your spouse to be strong. If you are intelligent, train your spouse to be intelligent. If you are bold, extend the courage to your spouse. If you are rich, don't rest until your spouse is financially independent. There is always going to be that moment when your only source of strength will come from your spouse. And whatever they have is what they will offer you at that point. Remember, God won't physically come down to help you.

The fight between husband and wife should never be a fight to finish. Domestic violence is real.

Understanding your spouse's weaknesses will help you to know when their error is uncontrollable or purposeful.

Some marriages are born out of revenge and bitterness. You are trying to prove to your ex that you can also have a home, then you settled for the next available man/woman.

A controlling spouse will always make you feel worthless without them. It is narcissistic

A spouse that envies and gets intimidated by your success doesn't deserve your lifetime.

Never misjudge loyalty as gullibility. If people are loyal to you, be honest with them.

Don't stay in an abusive marriage!

A peaceful marriage is another form of nourishment to the soul.

A bad marriage can eat you dry faster than cancer will.

If you want to swim across the ocean, your worry shouldn't be whether there would be sharks in the ocean. That's where they live.

The fact that you have forgiven someone doesn't mean they have repented of their sins. A loaded gun is always ready for execution.

Not all the fantasies we have about marriage are real.

God won't judge you based on your marital status but what you do with your marital status.

As you complain to your spouse about the things you don't like, don't forget to talk to God about it as well. The Holy Spirit will change your spouse better than nagging will do.

When metals keep unwanted dirt for too long, they stand a chance of being corrosive and eventually broken apart. Marriage is never a place to store up your grudges and malice; otherwise, it will not only be corrosive, it will be broken apart eventually.

If God wakes you up every morning, He isn't through with you yet.

That a situation is out of your control doesn't mean it is out of God's control.

The road the Lord is taking you through might be long and hard, but I tell you, the peace and the blessings that accompany it are without measure. Stay through with Him, He won't fail you.

Getting a confirmation from God doesn't mean we should run ahead of Him. A good intention with bad execution will always negate victory.

You can't hurry God.

Your spouse still doesn't know why you are angry, yet you keep punishing him/her. Are you God?

Take it or accept it, unforgiveness and peace of mind can never reign in the same marriage.

If it takes you a lifetime to forgive your spouse, who do you think would have lived a lifetime of a bitter marriage?

Tit for tat won't solve many problems in any marriage.

You can never have a happy marriage, if you keep bringing up stories of when your spouse hurt you in the past each time there is an argument.

Don't be so caught up with philosophy that you forget about God in your marriage. Philosophy guides, but God is the true manual of marriage.

The only product you will get from unforgiveness is bitterness and hatred.

At its best, marriage is still an option. You can become great in life with or without marriage.

Never assume you know everything about a spouse you haven't offended.

An honest opinion might not necessarily be the truth. One can be honestly wrong.

What gives you the assurance that the people you are seeking acceptance from accept themselves?

It is not fair to make your spouse pay for the errors of your ex.

Sometimes you go through painful moments, not because you are not smart enough to outwit it but just to teach you how to look at people in the valley with humility.

Every one of us goes into marriage with two things: expectations and baggage.

Your spouse is not always the real enemy of your marriage. Most times, they are just the bait the real enemy uses to frustrate you into committing marital errors. Don't bite the bait.

Don't fight your marital battle without knowing the root cause of the problem. If you don't know your enemy, you won't know what weapon to use to fight them.

If the best way you could describe your spouse is that they are foolish, guess what? That makes you a partner to a fool. And birds of a feather flock together.

If you are too shy to tell people how great your spouse is, then you will be a hypocrite if you suddenly have the courage to tell how bad he/she is when they misbehave.

A relationship you are not getting anything from is taking everything from you. Be smart.

Until we finally learn that we can't fit into every relationship, we won't have that absolute peace.

The approval/disapproval of a man is never a guarantee for your success or failure in life.

Marriage has the power to multiply whatever you sow into it, including hatred and love.

Okay, it is your in-law you are fighting, not your marriage. Don't mix up the fight.

Before you get mad at your in-laws, have you talked to your spouse about it? Your in-laws can't control your marriage without your spouse directly or indirectly giving them the access to it.

Your in-laws' influence on your marriage is an extension of their influence on their child.

If you lose the trust of a loyal friend to your moments of lies, your eventual moments of truth might not be enough to win back their trust.

If you take a marital advice from someone that constantly talks bad about their ex and the other gender, rest assured that your spouse will soon become an ex.

Don't get distracted fighting a battle that doesn't concern you. Not all the jabs thrown at you are worthy of your punches.

Three people make the rules in a marriage - the husband, the wife and God. All other input are just suggestions.

If we take away the pressure of religion, culture and tradition, a lot of broken marriages would still be existing.

Every argument is serious and every complaint deserves your listening ears, complacency is a threat to any relationship. Don't give it a chance.

ABOUT THE BOOK

Adesina David Okerinde and Mosebolatan Arinola Akande has been married for over a decade and are blessed with three beautiful children.

Adesina is a graduate of chemical engineering at Ladoke Akintola University of Technology (LAUTECH) Ogbomosho, and has a Masters in Environmental Engineering at Idaho State University, Idaho. He is also a veteran of the United States Army.

Mosebolatan is a graduate of computer science and Information technology at Bowen University, Iwo and her Bachelor of Science in Nursing at Idaho State University, Idaho.

They are both passionate about building beautiful marriages and relationships.

www.ingramcontent.com/pod-product-compliance
Lightning Source LLC
La Vergne TN
LVHW051847080426
835512LV00018B/3121